Someone from Assisi

by Thornton Wilder

A Samuel French Acting Edition

SAMUELFRENCH.COM
SAMUELFRENCH-LONDON.CO.UK

Copyright © 1957, 1961
Yale University, Fisk University and Oberlin College
Foreword copyright © 2014 by Tappan Wilder
All Rights Reserved

SOMEONE FROM ASSISI is fully protected under the copyright laws of the United States of America and all countries with which the United States has reciprocal copyright relations, whether through bilateral or multi-lateral treaties or otherwise, and including but not limited to, all countries covered by the Pan-American Copyright Convention, the Universal Copyright Convention, and the Berne Convention. All rights, including professional and amateur stage productions, recitation, lecturing, public reading, motion picture, radio broadcasting, television and the rights of translation into foreign languages are strictly reserved.

ISBN 978-0-573-70389-8

www.SamuelFrench.com
www.SamuelFrench-London.co.uk

FOR PRODUCTION ENQUIRIES

UNITED STATES AND CANADA
Info@SamuelFrench.com
1-866-598-8449

AMATEUR RIGHTS IN THE UNITED KINGDOM
Plays@SamuelFrench-London.co.uk
020-7255-4302

Each title is subject to availability from Samuel French, depending upon country of performance. Please be aware that *SOMEONE FROM ASSISI* may not be licensed by Samuel French in your territory. Producers should contact the nearest Samuel French office or licensing partner to verify availability.

For all enquiries regarding Professional productions in the United Kingdom; Professional and Amateur productions throughout the rest of Europe; and motion picture, television, and other media rights, please contact Alan Brodie Representation (Victoria@AlanBrodie.com). Visit www.thorntonwilder.com/contact for details.

CAUTION: Professional and amateur producers are hereby warned that *SOMEONE FROM ASSISI* is subject to a licensing fee. Publication of this play does not imply availability for performance. Professionals and Amateurs considering a production are strongly advised to apply for a license before starting rehearsals, advertising, or booking a theatre. A licensing fee must be paid whether the title is presented for charity or gain and whether or not admission is charged.

No one shall make any changes in this title for the purpose of production. No part of this book may be reproduced, stored in a retrieval system, or transmitted in any form, by any means, now known or yet to be invented, including mechanical, electronic, photocopying, recording, videotaping, or otherwise, without the prior written permission of the publisher. No one shall upload this title, or part of this title, to any social media websites.

MUSIC USE NOTE

Licensees are solely responsible for obtaining formal written permission from copyright owners to use copyrighted music in the performance of this play and are strongly cautioned to do so. If no such permission is obtained by the licensee, then the licensee must use only original music that the licensee owns and controls. Licensees are solely responsible and liable for all music clearances and shall indemnify the copyright owners of the play and their licensing agent, Samuel French, against any costs, expenses, losses and liabilities arising from the use of music by licensees. Please contact the appropriate music licensing authority in your territory for the rights to any incidental music.

IMPORTANT BILLING AND CREDIT REQUIREMENTS

All producers of *SOMEONE FROM ASSISI* must give credit to the author of the play in all programs distributed in connection with performances of the play, and in all instances in which the title of the play appears for the purposes of advertising, publicizing or otherwise exploiting the play and/ or a production. The name of the author must appear on a separate line on which no other name appears, immediately following the title and must appear in size of type not less than fifty percent of the size of the title type.

> This play may be performed only in its entirety. No permission can be granted for cuttings, readings or any use of parts of the play for any purpose whatsoever without the express written permission of the Wilder Family LLC. Absolutely *no* changes can be made to the text.

FOREWEORD TO WILDER'S
SOMEONE FROM ASSISI
The Sin of Lust

From the time he began dreaming up plays as a boy Thornton Wilder's vision of the theater transcended conventional boundaries, and to the end of his life his vision continually evolved and expanded. In 1956, he began work on what grew into an extravagantly ambitious project: two cycles of seven one-act plays based on the Deadly Sins and the Ages of Man. *Someone From Assisi* represents "Lust" in Wilder's projected cycle on the Seven Deadly Sins.

In what would prove to be his final dramatic works, Wilder sought not only to explore the theatrical possibilities inherent in the Sins and Ages, but (as he phrased it in his private journal on Christmas Day 1960) to "offer each play in the series as representing, also, a different mode of playwriting: Grand Guignol, Chekhov, Noh play, etc., etc." In short, he envisioned nothing less than a tour de force of dramatic theme and form encapsulated in the economy and intensity of the one-act play.

Wilder did not complete the challenge he set for himself, but he came close. The surviving work enriches his dramatic legacy and deserves to be remembered as more than a footnote to his lifelong conviction (written soon after *Our Town* opened on Broadway in 1938): "The theater offers to imaginative narration its highest possibilities."

The Sins and Ages Then and Now

A brief overview of the history of these plays will help readers place them in Wilder's career as a dramatist. Two Sins, *Bernice* (Pride) and *The Wreck on the 5:25* (Sloth), premiered in English at a special event in Berlin in 1957 (with Wilder performing in *Bernice*). For reasons that have never been clear, for he enjoyed the experience and felt that plays did well, he withdrew them. That same year a third Sin, *The Drunken Sisters* (Gluttony), written as the satyr play for Wilder's full length drama, *The Alcestiad*, proved successful in its premiere on the stage of Zürich's fabled Schauspielhaus.

Five years passed before the continuation of his ambitious scheme appeared on a stage in the United States. In January 1962, two new Ages (*Infancy* and *Childhood*) and a new Sin, *Someone From Assisi* (Lust), opened at Circle in the Square, then located off-Broadway on Bleecker Street, to the reported largest pre-opening advanced sale in that stage's then 11-year history. Billed as "Plays for Bleecker Street," the show of ran for 349 performances.

Then silence. After "Plays for Bleecker Street" closed, no more Sins or Ages appeared. When Thornton Wilder died in 1975 the public record of his 14-play scheme contained only four plays – two Ages (*Infancy* and *Childhood*) and two Sins (Lust and Gluttony).

Today, eleven of Wilder's Sins and Ages are available for production: a completed cycle of the seven Deadly Sins and four of seven Ages of Man. The source of the seven "new" plays is no secret. The missing pieces were found in Thornton Wilder's archives at Yale[1]. From this source, starting in 1995, his literary executor and family released the two plays withdrawn in 1957, *Cement Hands* (Avarice), and four additional titles (*Youth, The Rivers Under the Earth* [Middle Age][2], *A Ringing of Doorbells* [Envy] and *In Shakespeare and the Bible* [Wrath]) recovered and completed by the actor, director and friend of Wilder's, F.J. O'Neil. (Mr. O'Neil's valuable notes on the origin of each of these missing links follow the text of each play.)

The public reception of Thornton Wilder's long lost and new plays was gratifying. *The Wreck on the 5:25* was selected as one of the Best American Short Plays of 1994-95. In 1997, the Centenary of the playwright's birth, Kevin Kline starred in a premiere reading in New York of *Cement Hands*, and the works recovered by Mr. O'Neil served as the centerpieces of Actors Theatre of Louisville's 13th Annual Brown-Forman Classics in Context Festival.   Finally, as the capstone to the Centenary celebration, TCG Press in 1997 published the 11 Sins and Ages in Volume I of *The Collected Short Plays of Thornton Wilder.*

---

[1] No additional one-acts remain to be discovered in Thornton Wilder's archives at Yale.

[2] We believe Wilder intended *The Rivers Under the Earth* to represent Middle Age.

Wilder never followed conventional theatrical practice. As a young writer in his "Classic One Act Plays" of 1931, he swept away scenery and played provocative games with time and place. In the Sins and Ages, his farewell as a playwright, he is no less adventurous by way of settings, techniques, stage-craft and themes. One artistic trend of the day especially "fired his imagination" where these plays are concerned: his passionate belief in the value of the arena stage. "The boxed set play," he wrote in 1961, "encourages the anecdote…The unencumbered stage encourages the truth in everyone." Wilder felt so strongly that audiences should be seated as close to the actors as possible that Samuel French, for several years, was only permitted to license these plays to companies agreeing to perform them on a three-sided thrust or arena stage.

***

As part of its celebration of Wilder's one-act plays, Samuel French and the Wilder family take great pleasure in issuing new acting editions for the Sins and Ages long in print and, for the first time, acting editions of the seven new Wilder works. We invite those performing or teaching these plays to visit www.thorntonwilder.com for additional information.

– *Tappan Wilder,*
Literary Executor for Thornton Wilder

CHARACTERS

PICA, a twelve-year-old girl
MONA LUCREZIA, a crazy woman, forty
MOTHER CLARA, a sister at Saint Damian's, thirty-one
FATHER FRANCIS, a visiting priest, forty

SETTING

Poor Sisters Convent at Saint Damian's near Assisi.

*(The kitchen-garden behind the convent. A number of low benches surround the playing area. The actors' entrance at the back represents a door into the convent; it is framed by a trellis covered with vines. Opposite, the aisle through the audience represents a path to the village street. A young girl, **PICA**, twelve, barefoot and wearing a simple smock, comes running out of the convent; she stares down the aisle through the audience and starts to shout in anger and grief.)*

PICA. No! No! Old Crazy – go home! You mustn't come here today. Go home! Go HOME!! We have someone especially important coming and you mustn't be here! Go home! You'll spoil everything!

*(**MONA LUCRETIA**, looking much older than her forty years, comes lurching through the audience to the stage. She is crazy. Her black, gray and white hair is uncombed. She carries a large soiled shawl. She mumbles to herself as she advances.)*

MONA. Don't make such a noise, child. I must think what I'm going to say when he comes. Now, *you* go away. I must think.

PICA. No, *you* go away. – Oh, this is terrible!

*(**PICA** turns and rushes into the convent, calling:)*

Mother Clara! Mother Clara!

MONA. *(shouting)* It's I who have someone important coming – not you. And... *(worriedly)* I must be ready. It's so hard to be ready. I must put gold on my hair... and perfumes, more perfumes. He'll have elephants and...camels.

*(**MOTHER CLARA**, thirty-one, enters and stands at the convent door looking thoughtfully at **MONA LUCRETIA**. **PICA** passes her and comes toward the center of the stage.)*

PICA. Mother, she mustn't be here today when *he* comes. Tell old Thomas to drive her away. She'll sing and make a noise and spoil everything. – Old Crazy, *go home!* Mother Clara, we would die of shame, if *he* heard the things she says.

CLARA. *(quietly, her gaze on* **MONA***)* Be quiet, Pica. – Mona, do you know me? – What is her name, Pica?

PICA. I don't know. I've forgotten.

CLARA. Go and ask Old Thomas what her name is. I don't want you to call her Old Crazy. – Has she a home to go to?

PICA. Oh, Mother – she is very rich. But her family drives her out of the house all day.

*(***MONA*** has seated herself on one of the benches, her elbows on her knees. She is staring at the ground.)*

CLARA. Go and find out what her name is.

*(***PICA*** runs into the convent.)*

Mona, do you know me?...Mona, do you know me? I am Mother Clara of the Poor Sisters at Saint Damian's. Do you know me?...What is your name?

MONA. *(rising; impressively)* I am who I am. – *He* is coming today. You know I am the Queen of...

CLARA. What?...Who is coming?

MONA. The King of...

CLARA. Yes. What king?

MONA. *(becoming confused)* The King of Solomon. To see me. I must be ready. He is coming...from France. And...

CLARA. From France?!!

MONA. Of course, from France. I must have presents to give him. And...He will have lions. And...

CLARA. Yes. You must be ready, Mona.

(In order to induce **MONA** *to leave the garden,* **CLARA** *crosses the stage and starts walking backward through the audience.)*

CLARA. Come. You must go to your home and make yourself ready. Look!…Just look! You must comb your hair beautifully. And you must *wash your face*! – Who is it you say is coming?

MONA. *(following her; angrily)* I *told* you – the King of Solomon…Of France. That is: French France. I didn't *love* him – *no!*; but he loved me. But now he has become a great person and he sends me all these messages.

(Stopping at the edge of the stage, She looks at the floor in a troubled way; softly:)

Did I tell you the truth? Did I love him? Did I? – Oh, he wrote such songs for me. Songs and songs.

CLARA. Come, Mona. I think you should rest, too.

MONA. *(confidentially)* If I walk slowly he will not see that I am lame. One of the boys in the street kicked me.

CLARA. Kicked…!! Yes, walk slowly. Like a queen. No, no, stand up straight, Mona – like a queen. You can do it. Come. What will you say when you see the king?

MONA. I shall say…*(standing straight)* Oh, King of Solomon, I shall say: Change the world!

CLARA. *(astonished)* You will say that?

MONA. They throw stones at me. They kick me. Everywhere people hate people. My daughters – with brooms – they drive me away. I can't go home; I can only go home when the sun goes down. And I shall say oh, King, change the hearts of the world.

CLARA. *(returns to the stage; as* **MONA** *passes her on the way to the village)* That is a very good thing to say. You won't forget it?

MONA. *(loudly)* The world is *bad*.

CLARA. Yes.

MONA. Nobody is kind anymore.

CLARA. You tell your daughters that Mother Clara of Saint Damian's says that they are to let you into the house; and you will wash your face and your hair, won't you? And God bless you, dear Mona, and make you wise… wise and beautiful…for your friend.

(MONA has almost disappeared. From the convent sounds of joyous cries and laughter. PICA comes running out like an arrow.)

PICA. *(shrilly)* He has come, Mother Clara. Father Francis is here!

(She flies back into the convent.)

MONA. *(returning a few steps)* What did you say?...Wise?

CLARA. Yes...and beautiful. Good-bye, Mona. Remember. Good-bye.

MONA. *(mumbling)* Wise...and beautiful...

(She goes out.)

(FRANCIS appears at the convent door. He is forty, browned by the weather, almost blind, and with very few teeth. Also he is very happy. CLARA, joyously, and as lightly as a young girl, runs to the center of the stage and falls on her knees.)

CLARA. Bless me, Father.

FRANCIS. *(kneels, facing her)* God bless you, dearest Sister, with all His love. – And now you bless me, Sister.

CLARA. *(lowered eyes, laughing protest)* Father!

FRANCIS. Say after me God bless you, Brother Francis, and God forgive you that load of sins with which you have offended Him.

CLARA. God bless you, Brother Francis, with all His love.

FRANCIS. And...

CLARA. *(rippling laughter of protest)* I cannot say that, Father.

FRANCIS. I order you by your holy obedience.

CLARA. ...And God forgive you that load of sins Father! – with which you have offended Him. – There!

FRANCIS. Yes.

(They both stay on their knees a moment, looking at one another, radiantly. FRANCIS rises first and says with a touch of earnest injunction.)

I want you to say that prayer...that *whole* prayer...for me, every day.

CLARA. I will, Father. – Now sit in the sun. The meal will be ready very soon.

FRANCIS. *(sitting)* And how is my little plant?

CLARA. *(again soft running laughter)* Your little plant is very well, Father.

FRANCIS. Let me see…was it ten years ago we cut off your beautiful hair and found you a bridegroom?

CLARA. Ten years ago next month.

FRANCIS. Yes…Never, Sister Clara, have I seen a more beautiful wedding…

CLARA. *(blushing with pleasure)* Father!

FRANCIS. *(softly)* …Except, of course, my own.

CLARA. Oh, yes – *yours*. We know all about that – to the Lady Poverty.

FRANCIS. The Lady Poverty.

CLARA. Yes. – And how are *you*, dear Father?

FRANCIS. Well…Well…

CLARA. And your eyes?

FRANCIS. Oh, Sister…I can see the path. I can see the brothers and sisters. I can see the Crucified on the wall.

CLARA. Oh, then, I'm so happy. I'd heard that you had some difficulty.

FRANCIS. *(emphatically)* Oh, yes, I can *see*. *(confidentially)* Maybe I'm a little bit blind; but…I *hear* so well. I *hear* so much better.

CLARA. Do you?

FRANCIS. Everything talks all the time. The trees. And the water. And the stones.

CLARA. *(holding her breath)* What, Father?

FRANCIS. The stones. The rocks. Now, when I go up there to pray, I must say to them: "Be quiet."

CLARA. "Be quiet."

FRANCIS. "Be quiet for a while." And they are quiet.

CLARA. Yes, Father.

(There is a moment while she digests this; then she begins again with animation.)

My sisters are so happy that you have come. Sister Agnes has made something for you. Now promise that you will eat all of it. It will break her heart if you don't.

FRANCIS. All?

CLARA. *(laughing)* Oh, it is very little. We have learned that.

FRANCIS. All? My stomach has grown so small... *(making a ring with his thumb and forefinger)* ...That is enough.

CLARA. We understand. But this time there is a touch – a touch of saffron.

FRANCIS. Saffron!!

CLARA. The Count sent it to us from the castle, especially for you. He remembered that you liked it...*before*...

FRANCIS. Before? Before when?

CLARA. Well...Father...before...Before you entered the religious life.

FRANCIS. *(agitated)* Before!!? When I was the most sinful of men! No, no, Sister Clara! Go quickly and tell Sister Agnes – no saffron! No saffron.

CLARA. *(calling sharply and clapping her hands)* Pica! Pica!

*(**PICA** enters at once.)*

PICA. Yes, Mother.

CLARA. Tell Sister Agnes *no* saffron in Father's dish. And do not stand by the door.

PICA. Yes, Mother.

*(During this interchange, **MONA** has returned, mumbling, through the audience.)*

MONA. They throw stones at me. They kick me. Hmm. But when the king comes they will learn who I am. Hmm. They will sing another song.

CLARA. *(her eyes again thoughtfully on* **MONA***, who has seated herself on one of the benches)* She has lost her wits…She comes of a prosperous family, but they send her out of the house all day. I think the children torment her. She likes to come and sit here, rain or shine. – Father – she thinks she is the Queen of Sheba! And that King Solomon is coming to visit her!

FRANCIS. *(delighted)* She thinks she is…! How rich she is. How happy she must be!

CLARA. *(pointing to her own forehead)* Yes – but she is touched.

FRANCIS. Touched?…Oh, touched. – Is she able to receive the blessed sacrament?

CLARA. No. I think not. They tell me that in church she cries out and says unsuitable things. No, she is not allowed in the church.

FRANCIS. What is her name?

CLARA. Everyone here seems to have forgotten it. They simply call her Old Crazy. We call her Mona.

FRANCIS. *(taking a few steps toward* **MONA***)* Mona!…Yes, your king is coming.

MONA. *(violently)* Go away from me! I know all about your nasty filthy wicked ways!

CLARA. *(authoritatively)* Now, Mona, you must be quiet or we will send you away – with a broom, too. You know our Thomas. Our Thomas knows how to make you move.

FRANCIS. *(quiets* **CLARA** *with a gesture; his eyes on* **MONA** *in reflection)* Who can measure the suffering – the waste – in the world? And every being born into the world – except One – has added to it. You and I have made it more and more.

(He turns to **CLARA** *and adds with eager face:)*

Let us go to the church now and fall on our knees. Let us ask forgiveness.

CLARA. Father, we shall go to the church later. Now you have come here to take the noon meal with my dear sisters.

FRANCIS. *(with a sigh, as of a pleasure postponed)* Yes...yes.

CLARA. *(resuming the animated tone)* You received my letter? We can't give thanks enough! More and more are coming all the time. Sometimes I'm at my wit's end to find room and food for all these girls and women who are coming to join us. Oh, but I won't trouble you with *those* things – beds and food. We always find a way.

FRANCIS. Yes. Yes. No one would believe how we always find more beds and food.

CLARA. And their happiness! From morning to night. – You will hear them sing. They have been learning some new music to sing to you.

FRANCIS. *(rising, stuttering with eagerness)* Sister C-C-Clara, let us go into the chapel and thank God.

CLARA. We will. We will. But now, dear Father, just for a moment, let us sit in the sun and rest ourselves.

FRANCIS. *(again resigned)* ...Yes...Very well.

CLARA. Father, there is something I've long wanted to ask you. Can we talk for a moment of childish things? – Father, you will eat the noonday meal at our table today? You will?

FRANCIS. Sister! Sister! Can't I have it out here? *Where* I eat it is of no importance. I shall see the sisters later when I preach to them.

CLARA. Father, you hurt them.

FRANCIS. Hurt them?! I hurt them?

CLARA. They cannot understand it. You let Brother Avisio and Brother Juniper eat with us.

FRANCIS. Yes...yes...

CLARA. But you have never sat down with us at our table... Why is that? *(lowering her voice)* My sisters are beginning to believe that you think that women are of a *lower order* in God's love.

FRANCIS. Sister Clara!!

CLARA. They have heard that you share your meal with... wolves and birds, but never with *them*. – Can the Father Francis whom we love – this once – sit down with us women?

FRANCIS. *(agitated slightly but compliant)* Yes…oh, yes…I will.

CLARA. *(urgently)* It is so important, Father. I work among these good women and girls. They have left everything. They have God in Heaven but they have very little on earth. *(He nods repeatedly.)* Thank you! Now there's another childish thing I want to ask you. Brother Avisio told me a short time ago that you were christened John. Is that true?

FRANCIS. Yes. Yes. John.

CLARA. You chose the name Francis?

FRANCIS. My friends gave it to me. But that's long ago.

MONA. *(from under the hood of her shawl, as though brooding to herself)* Francis the Frenchman…They all called him that. That's what I called him, too.

*(after **FRANCIS** and **CLARA** have looked at **MONA** a moment)*

FRANCIS. Long ago – when I was a young man. Before I found something better, I was never tired of hearing all those songs and stories that came down from France…about knights in armor who went about the world killing dragons and tyrants. A growing boy must have something to admire – to make his heart swell. I talked about those stories to everyone I knew. I dressed myself in foreign dress. I made songs, too – many of them. And…but…

CLARA. Why do you stop, Father?

FRANCIS. And I heard that each of these knights had a lady. *(He looks at her with pain and appeal.)* I looked everywhere. I…I…looked everywhere.

CLARA. Do not talk of it, if it distresses you.

FRANCIS. *(low and urgently)* …May God forgive me that load of sin with which I offended him!

CLARA. Yes.

FRANCIS. I went through a troubled time… *(Suddenly, he looks at her happily.)* And then I found my lady.

CLARA. *(laughing)* Yes, we know, Father.

FRANCIS. Poverty! And I married her!

CLARA. Yes.

FRANCIS. And ever since, I go about the world singing her praises.

CLARA. Yes.

FRANCIS. *(eagerly)* Before I knew her I was a coward. Yes. I was afraid of everything: of going into the forests at night; I was afraid of hunger and of cold. I was afraid to knock at the doors of nobles and great people. But *now* – with *her* beside me – I go everywhere. I do not trouble when I go into the Pope's presence, even. I am not afraid when twenty new brothers arrive at our house: where shall I put them? How shall I feed them? She shows me.

*(***CLARA** *nods in complete agreement.)*

But how can one say how beautiful she is! And …. and *(lowering his voice)* how severe. Sometimes I almost offend her. And then I know that her eyes are *turned away* from me!… *(suddenly raising his hands)* No saffron! No saffron! – But most of the time we live together in great happiness.

(He crosses the stage, groping in his memory for an old song.)

…That song…that old song I wrote for her:

When in the darkness of the night
I see no lantern and no star,
My lady's eyes will bring me light.
When in pathless woods I stray
My feet have stumbled in despair
My lady's eyes will show the way.

MONA. When prison chains do fetter me –

FRANCIS. *(a loud cry of recognition)* Mona Lucrezia!!

MONA. *(harshly)* Shame on you! To sing that song in the ears of a holy woman! *That* is Mother Clara of Saint Damian's. Cover your ears, Mother Clara. *(advancing on* **FRANCIS***)* What do you know of Francis the

Frenchman? *I* know him. He wrote that song for me.

When prison chains do fetter me
And it is written I must die
My lady's eyes will set me free.

Yes, we all knew that he searched for his lady. We all knew that – the mayor's wife and Ninina Dono…and I…

FRANCIS. Mona Lucrezia. *(trembling, to* **CLARA***)* Leave me alone with her.

MONA. Mother Clara, they say that he goes all over the world now; that he sees the Pope and says good morning, good morning; that he's gone to Palestine to convert the Grand Turk himself –

CLARA. Do not be long, Father. The meal is almost ready.

(She hurries out.)

MONA. *(calling after her)* He said my body was of marble and snow – no, he said that my body was of fire and snow.

(She starts leaving the stage through the audience.)

He'll convert the Grand Turk. The Devil will help him. He converted the mayor's wife and me – the Devil helping him.

*(***FRANCIS***, shaken and speechless, stands looking after her.* **PICA** *has entered stealthily from the convent.* **FRANCIS** *appears not to hear her.)*

PICA. Father Francis, we did everything we could to prevent that crazy woman from coming here today. Mother Clara says that you are going to sit at table with the sisters – for the first time. You must sit quite still during the reading because Sister John of the Nails is going to draw a picture of you that we can have on the wall. When people draw you, you have to sit very still, because when you move, they can't see what to draw – *(sounds of shouting from the street)*

MONA. *(offstage)* Go away from me! Peter, put down that stone! Aiiiiiiee!

PICA. Oh, Father Francis! She's coming back again. They've been throwing stones at her.

(She goes down the aisle.)

Don't...come...back. We'll beat you!

FRANCIS. Come here and be quiet!

*(**MONA** lurches back, shouting toward the street. One side of her face is covered with blood. She is struck again and sinks on one knee at the edge of the stage.)*

MONA. Pigs – all of you. Lock your mothers up and there'll be no more of you.

FRANCIS. Come and sit down here, Mona Lucrezia.

MONA. *(to **FRANCIS**)* Don't strike me – you! Go away from me.

FRANCIS. *(authoritatively to **PICA**)* Get a bowl of water and a clean cloth. Put some leaves and stems of the hazel into it. And be quick.

*(**PICA** stands gaping.)*

Be quick! Be quick!

*(**PICA** runs off.)*

MONA. *(harshly to **FRANCIS**)* You kicked me!

FRANCIS. No, Mona Lucrezia.

MONA. You did.

FRANCIS. Come over here and sit down. You are among friends now.

MONA. *(sitting down)* There are no friends. I don't want any friends. I had some.

*(She stares at **FRANCIS**, somberly.)*

Who are you? What's your name?

FRANCIS. I was christened John.

MONA. John! – Do you know who John was?

FRANCIS. *(in a small voice)* Yes.

MONA. You stand there – idle as a log – and *do* nothing. If all the men in the world named John would join themselves together and be worthy of their name, the world would not be like that.

FRANCIS. Don't put your hand on your wound, Lucrezia. We'll wash it in a moment.

MONA. *(harshly)* Don't talk to me! *(silence) (then broodingly to herself)* The king will look for me. "Where is my queen?" I'll hide where he can't find me. – And I had something to tell him.

*(**CLARA** enters swiftly with water and a cloth. She kneels before **MONA**.)*

CLARA. Hold your face up, Mona Lucrezia.

MONA. Don't touch me! You are a holy woman. I will do it myself. Or let that log do it – that worthless John.

*(As though overcoming a powerful repulsion, **FRANCIS** applies the wet cloth to **MONA**'s forehead.)*

MONA. *(striking him)* That hurts.

FRANCIS. Yes, it will hurt for a minute. Sit quiet. Sit quiet.

MONA. *(with a sob, but submitting)* That hurts.

*(At a signal from **FRANCIS**, **CLARA** leaves.)*

FRANCIS. There, that's better. Now your hands…

MONA. *(with closed eyes)* They wash the dead. They washed us when we were born.

(silence)

FRANCIS. Now your face again.

MONA. No! Don't touch me again. I don't like to be touched.

(She takes the cloth.)

(grumbling as though to herself) On an important day like this!…And you one of those great good-for-nothing monks, filling your big belly with meals at other people's tables. *(directly at him, fiercely)* God must weep!

FRANCIS. Yes.

MONA. Francis the Frenchman became a monk. I knew him. I never said to him what I should have said. It was clear in my mind, like writing on the wall; but I never said it. Whatever Francis the Frenchman wanted to do, oh, he did it. His will was like…! It was that that made us break our vows. I had never deceived my husband. I told him I was afraid of God. What do you suppose he said? I told him I was afraid of losing God's love. *(She stares at him.)* He said: all love is one!

FRANCIS. No-o!

MONA. He said that he would make me the lady of his life and that he would do anything that I ordered him to do…I should have ordered him to do…that though that was like writing on the wall. Even then, though I was a girl, I knew that the world was a valley without rain…a city without food. I knew…I felt…he could… *(She becomes confused.)*

FRANCIS. *(low)* What would you have said, Lucrezia?

MONA. *(rising)* I shall be your lady. And I command you: OWN NOTHING. No one will listen to you, if you have a roof over your head. No one will listen to you if you know where you will eat tomorrow. It is fear that has driven love out of the world and only a man without fear can bring it back. *(She glares at him a moment, then sinks back on the bench.)* But I never said it!

FRANCIS. Lucrezia, do you know me? I am Francis.

MONA. *(without interest)* No, you are some other Francis. I am going now.

FRANCIS. *(calling)* Pica! Pica!

MONA. *(starting to the town)* I'm tired…but I'm afraid of the butcher's dog…and the mayor's –

FRANCIS. Pica!

(PICA rushes in.)

I am taking Mona Lucrezia to her home. *(He indicates with his eyes.)* I will need you to show me the way.

PICA. Father Francis, the sisters are ready to sit down at the table. You will break their hearts.

MONA. *(starting)* I had a stick. The boys are always taking away my stick. *(stopping)* Someone was coming to town today…

PICA. *(spitefully)* Yes! Father Francis himself. And you've spoiled everything!

FRANCIS. *(to PICA)* Hsh! – I cannot see the path. Give me your hand.

MONA. *(turning)* Those dogs – the butcher's Rufus. Brother John, haven't you got a stick?

PICA. *(giggling)* She doesn't even know that dogs don't bite Father Francis!

MONA. *(stopping and peering at FRANCIS)* Haven't you got a stick?

FRANCIS. No, Mona Lucrezia. I have nothing.

(They go out.)

End of Play

THORNTON WILDER (1897-1975) was an accomplished novelist and playwright whose works explore the connection between the commonplace and the cosmic dimensions of human experience. He won three Pulitzer Prizes: for his novel *The Bridge of San Luis Rey*, and two plays, *Our Town* and *The Skin of Our Teeth*. Wilder's farce, *The Matchmaker*, was adapted as the musical *Hello, Dolly!* He also enjoyed enormous success as a translator, adaptor, actor, librettist and lecturer/teacher. Wilder's many honors include the Gold Medal for Fiction from the American Academy of Arts and Letters and the Presidential Medal of Freedom. Penelope Niven's definitive biography, *Thornton Wilder: A Life*, was published in October 2012. For more information, please visit www.thorntonwilder.com.

Also by
Thornton Wilder...

The Alcestiad

The Beaux' Stratagem (with Ken Ludwig)

The Matchmaker

Our Town

The Skin of Our Teeth

<u>Thornton Wilder One Act Series: The Ages of Man</u>

Infancy

Childhood

Youth

The Rivers Under the Earth

<u>Thornton Wilder One Act Series: Wilder's Classic One Acts</u>

The Long Christmas Dinner

Queens of France

Pullman Car Hiawatha

Love and How to Cure It

Such Things Only Happen in Books

The Happy Journey to Trenton and Camden

<u>Thornton Wilder One Act Series: The Seven Deadly Sins</u>

The Drunken Sisters

Bernice

The Wreck on the 5:25

A Ringing of Doorbells

In Shakespeare and the Bible

Someone From Assisi

Cement Hands

Please visit our website **samuelfrench.com** for complete descriptions and licensing information.

www.ingramcontent.com/pod-product-compliance
Lightning Source LLC
Chambersburg PA
CBHW071419290426
44108CB00014B/1886